PRAISE FOR *YOUR ILLUSTRATED GUIDE TO BECOMING ONE WITH THE UNIVERSE*

"*Your Illustrated Guide to Becoming One with the Universe* opens your mind to the infinite possibilities that exist within yourself. Yumi Sakugawa adds new life to age-old wisdom through her dreamlike drawings. I am a huge fan of Yumi's work!"
—Mallika Chopra, founder and CEO of Intent.com

"I keep this little book beside my bed to remind me of everything I know, but often forget."
—Pam Grout, author of *E-Cubed* and *E-Squared*

"In the deepest crystal caves of my heart is a voice, a voice bejeweled with squiggly star shapes and amorphous beings, a strange voice that sings to me in the quietest of moments. Sometimes when that voice is missing, *Your Illustrated Guide to Becoming One with the Universe* takes its place. Yumi channels this voice effortlessly, and her illustrated guide has time and time again become my lullaby, my friend-love, and a sentient being dressed in the most effortless beeline black lines and jewels of wisdom. I LOVE THIS."
—Shilo Shiv Suleman, visual artist and creator of The Fearless Collective

YOUR ILLUSTRATED GUIDE TO BECOMING ONE WITH THE UNIVERSE

YUMI SAKUGAWA

▲adamsmedia

Published by
Adams Media, a division of F+W Media, Inc.
57 Littlefield Street, Avon, MA 02322. U.S.A.
www.adamsmedia.com

ISBN 10: 1-4405-8263-7
ISBN 13: 978-1-4405-8263-9
eISBN 10: 1-4405-8264-5
eISBN 13: 978-1-4405-8264-6

Printed in the United States of America.

10 9 8 7 6 5

Illustrated by Yumi Sakugawa.
Cover by Yumi Sakugawa.

This book is available at quantity discounts for bulk purchases.
For information, please call 1-800-289-0963.

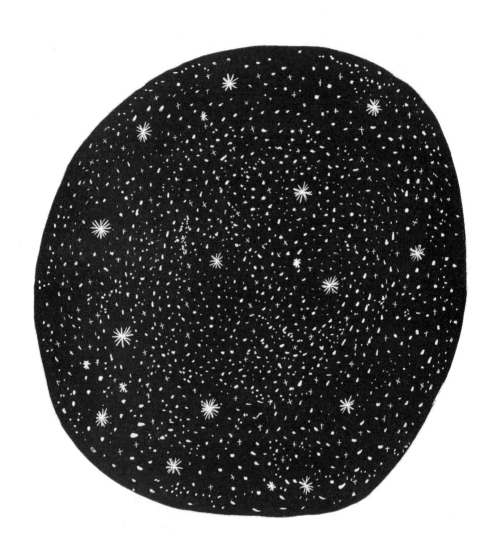

YOU DON'T LIKE YOUR LIFE RIGHT NOW

YOU CAN'T GET OVER THINGS THAT HAPPENED IN THE PAST

YOU ARE ANGRY AT YOURSELF, SOMEONE, OR THE WORLD

YOU FEEL LIKE THE UNIVERSE DEALT YOU A BAD HAND

YOU FEEL LIKE OTHER PEOPLE HAVE IT BETTER THAN YOU DO

YOU ARE WAITING FOR AN IDEALIZED, PERFECT FUTURE TO ARRIVE

BLAH, BLAH, BLAH...

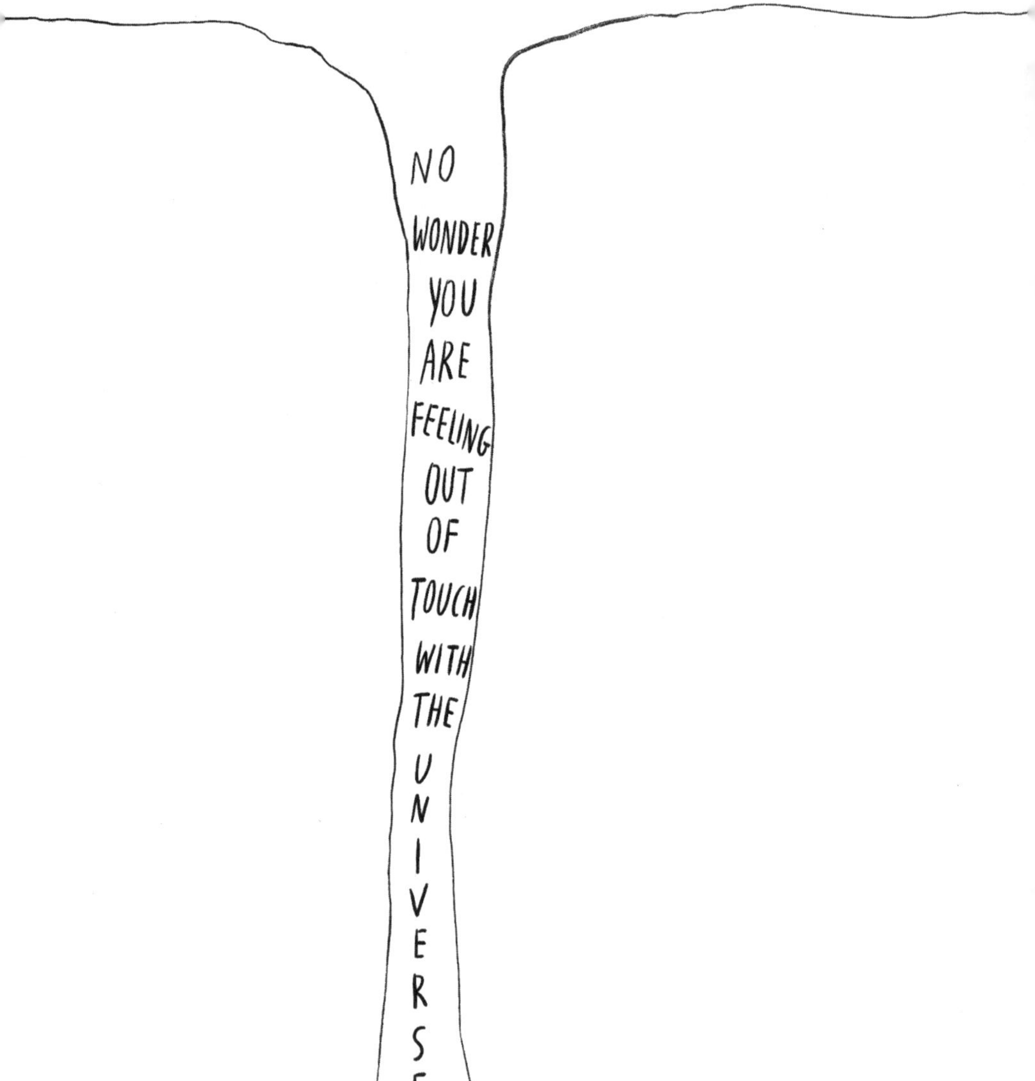
NO WONDER YOU ARE FEELING OUT OF TOUCH WITH THE UNIVERSE.....

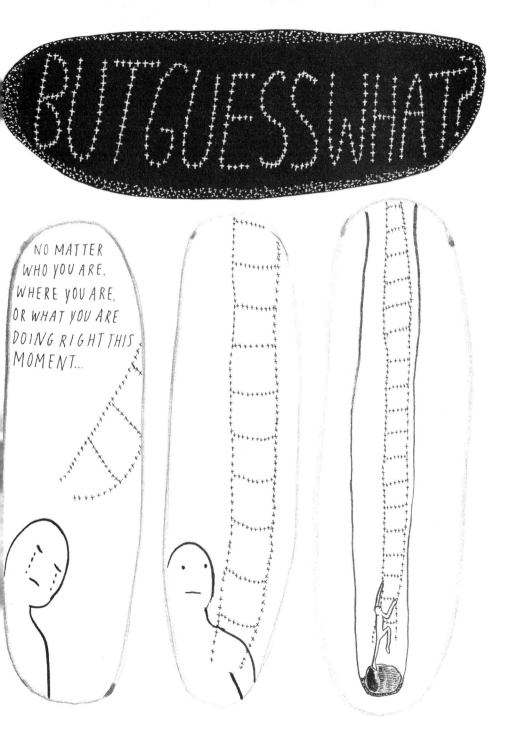

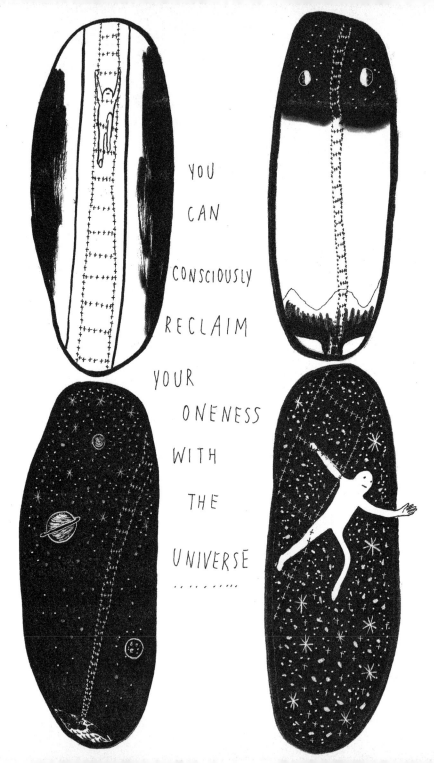

YOU CAN CONSCIOUSLY RECLAIM YOUR ONENESS WITH THE UNIVERSE ....

.....AND
EXPERIENCE
TRUE JOY

SO WHAT ARE YOU WAITING FOR?

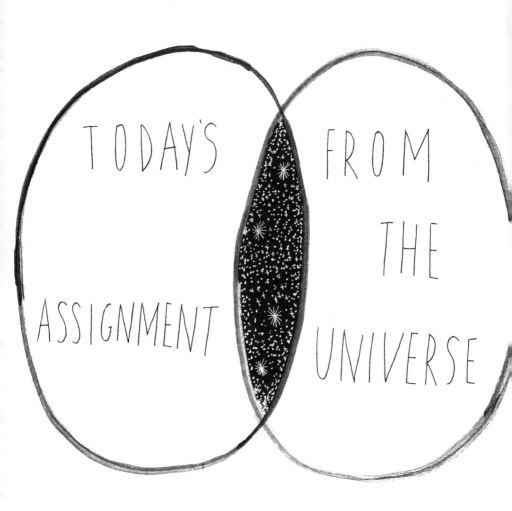

LET THE UNIVERSE KNOW THAT YOU
WANT TO GET TO KNOW THE
UNIVERSE/YOURSELF MORE

TONIGHT, LIE DOWN UNDER
THE OPEN NIGHT SKY.

hello UNIVERSE
i would like to
CONNECT with
you......

SEND A TELEPATHIC MESSAGE OUT INTO THE
NIGHT SKY, THE STARS, DISTANT GALAXIES,
FARAWAY PLANETS, AND EVERYTHING
AROUND YOU

SOONER
OR LATER
YOU WILL RECEIVE

A RESPONSE BACK
FROM THE UNIVERSE

LESSON 2
PAY ATTENTION AND LISTEN
(EMPTINESS IS EVERYTHING)

MOST OF THE TIME

THE UNIVERSE SPEAKS
TO US

VERY QUIETLY

IN POCKETS
OF SILENCE

IN COINCIDENCES

IN NATURE

IN FORGOTTEN
MEMORIES

IN THE SHAPE
OF CLOUDS

IN MOMENTS
OF SOLITUDE

IN SMALL
TUGS AT OUR
HEARTS

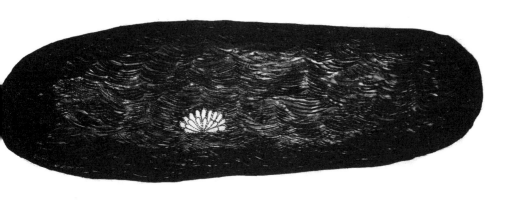

WHEN WE COMPLETELY CALM THE MURKY WAVES OF OUR MIND
TO TRULY PAY ATTENTION AND LISTEN, WE CAN CLEARLY
SEE WHAT IS REFLECTED ABOVE...

SO FOR THE NEXT FEW DAYS AND FOR THE REST OF YOUR LIFE...

PAY ATTENTION AND LISTEN

YOUR ASSIGNMENT
FROM THE UNIVERSE

CONNECT YOUR
HEART TO AN
ANTENNA THAT
PICKS UP INVISIBLE
FREQUENCIES FROM
THE UNIVERSE

WHAT ARE SOME
SECRET MESSAGES
YOU HAVE BEEN
MISSING THIS
ENTIRE TIME?

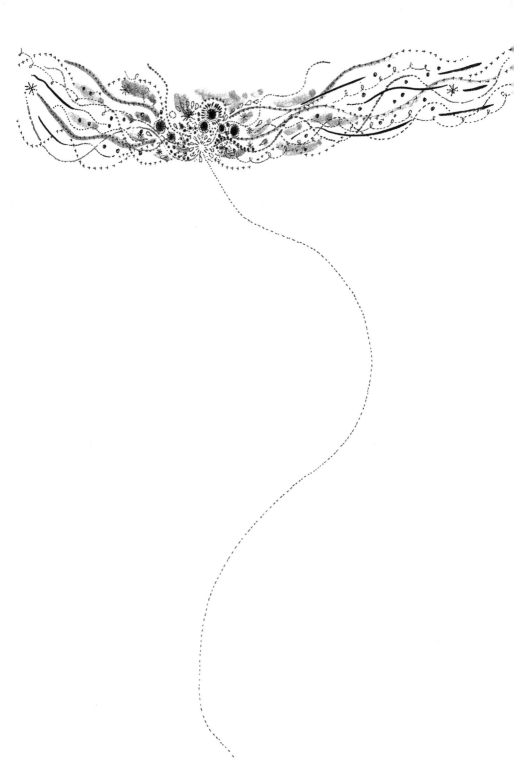

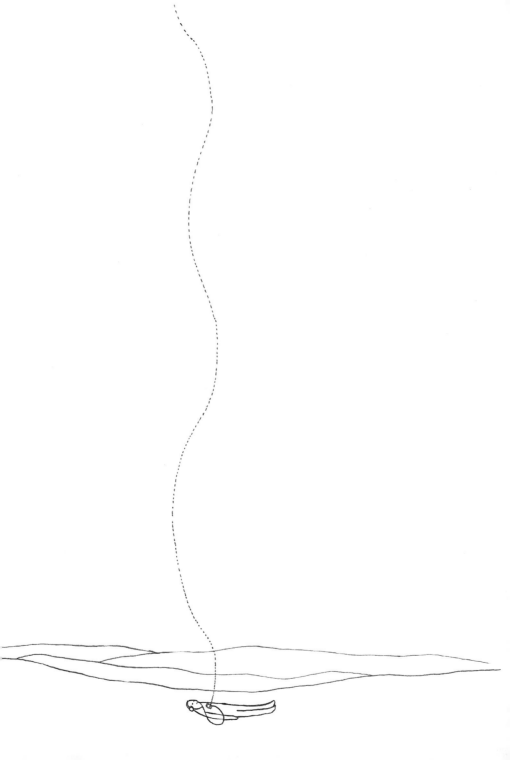

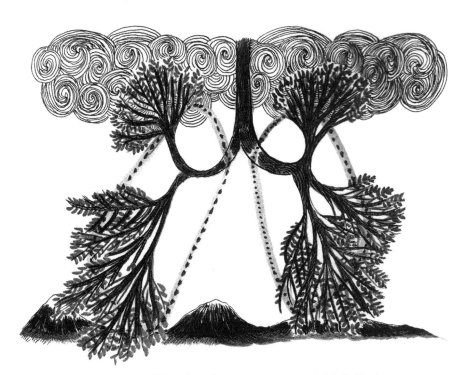

LET US GET REACQUAINTED WITH THE MIRACLE THAT IS

your breath

ALL THE TREES, FLOWERS, AND PLANTS ON THIS EARTH MAKE IT POSSIBLE FOR YOU TO BREATHE. ALL LIVING THINGS ON THIS EARTH ARE BREATHING IN AND BREATHING OUT THE SAME AIR THAT YOU ARE.

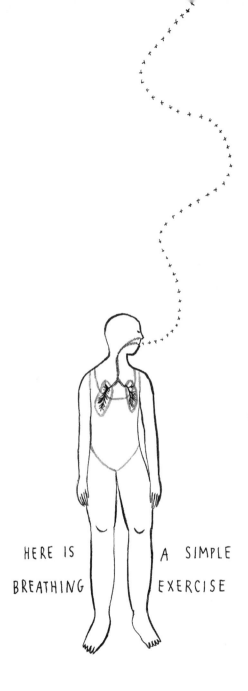

HERE IS A SIMPLE BREATHING EXERCISE

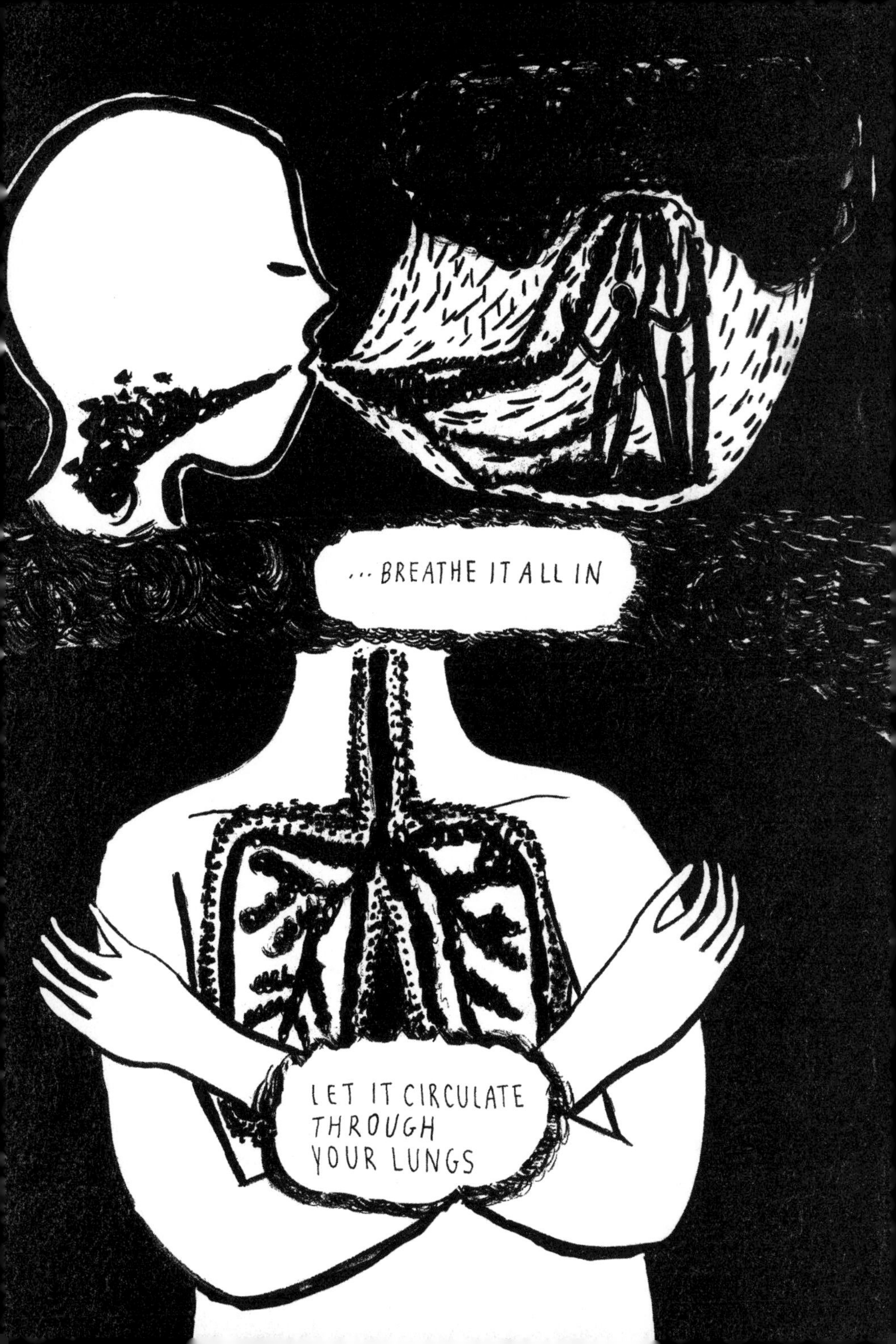
... BREATHE IT ALL IN
LET IT CIRCULATE THROUGH YOUR LUNGS

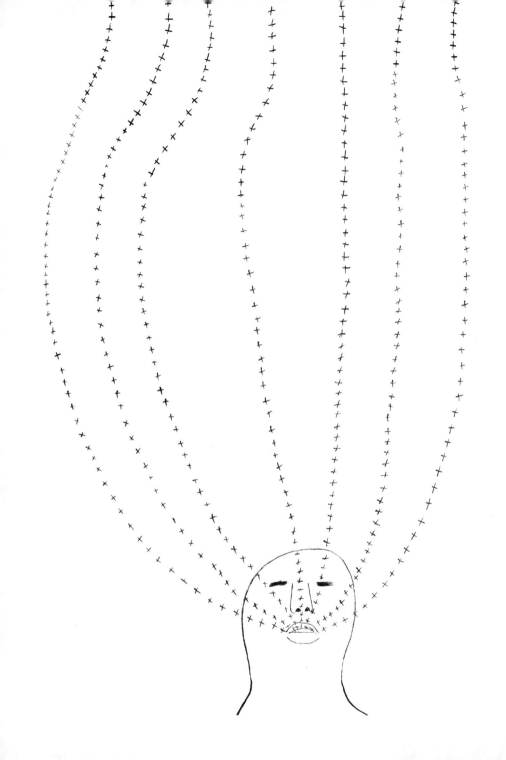

JUST

REMEMBER

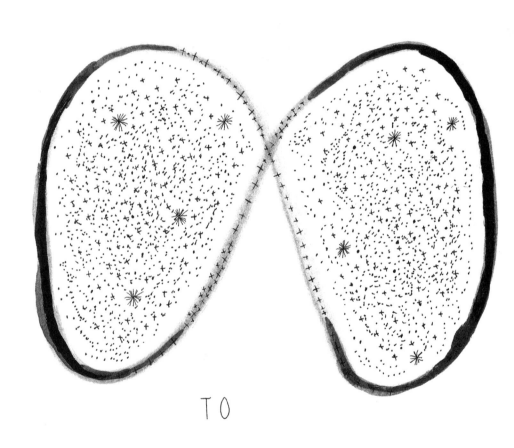

TO

BREATHE

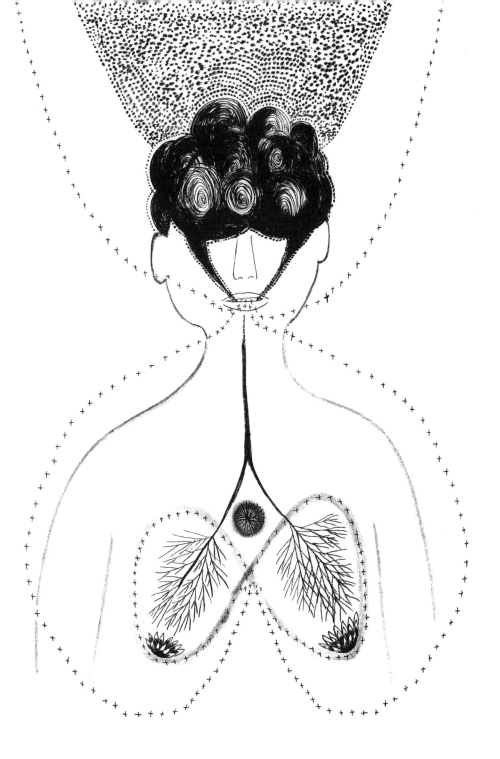

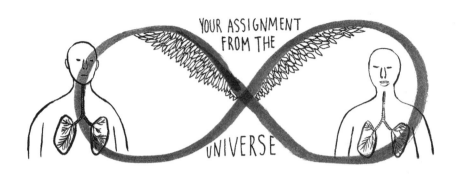

RELEASE IT INTO THE SKY

AND WATCH IT DISAPPEAR
INTO THE CLOUDS

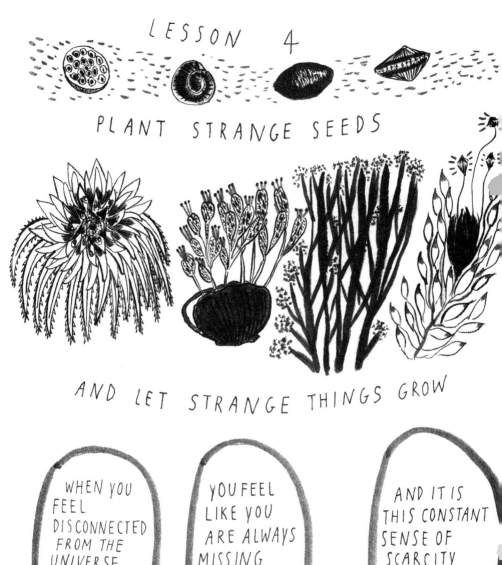

LESSON 4

PLANT STRANGE SEEDS

AND LET STRANGE THINGS GROW

WHEN YOU FEEL DISCONNECTED FROM THE UNIVERSE

YOU FEEL LIKE YOU ARE ALWAYS MISSING SOMETHING OR LACKING SOMETHING

AND IT IS THIS CONSTANT SENSE OF SCARCITY THAT MAKES YOU UNHAPPY

HERE IS ONE
SECRET TO FEEL
ONE WITH THE
UNIVERSE:

RATHER THAN
WAITING FOR
THE UNIVERSE
TO PROVIDE FOR
YOU...

...PLANT
SOME STRANGE
SEEDS ON YOUR
OWN WITH YOUR OWN
TWO HANDS

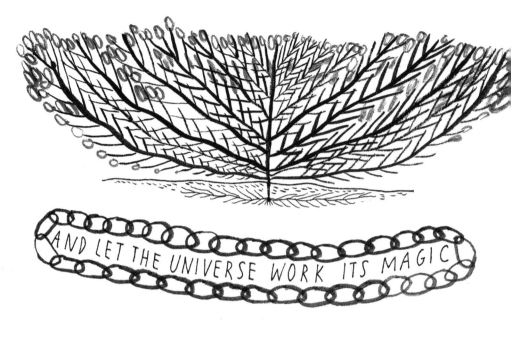

AND LET THE UNIVERSE WORK ITS MAGIC

STEP ONE

GATHER THE STRANGEST, MOST MYSTERIOUS, AND MOST BEAUTIFU SEEDS YOU CAN GET YOUR HANDS ON

THESE SEEDS CAN CONTAIN

A CRAZY SECRET
DREAM TO TRANSFORM
THE WORLD

A SIMPLE DESIRE
TO BE MORE AT PEACE

YOUR NEXT BIG IDEA

BIG ADVENTURES

UNEXPECTED,
DELIGHTFUL OPPORTUNITIES

SUPER-SECRET
DREAM X

ONCE YOU HAVE GATHERED
YOUR SEEDS, GO JOURNEY TO
SOME DEEP AND WILD SPACE
WHERE NO ONE CAN SEE YOU

AND PLANT THOSE SEEDS

DEEP

INTO

THE

EARTH

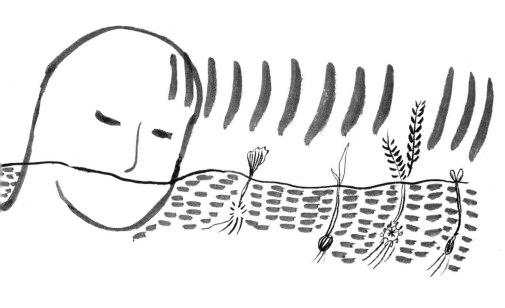

WHILE YOU ARE
WAITING FOR YOUR STRANGE
SEEDS TO GROW... *SEND TELEPATHIC MESSAGES OF ENCOURAGEMENT, LOVE, AND ATTENTION.*

LET GO OF ALL RIGID EXPECTATIONS OF HOW
THESE SEEDS WILL GROW AND WHAT THEY W.
GROW INTO

SOME SEEDS STAY HIDDEN IN THE EARTH FOREVER

THAT'S OKAY. THEY JUST WEREN'T MEANT TO BE.

SOME SEEDS GROW INTO STRANGE TREES, BLOOM INTO STRANGE FLOWERS

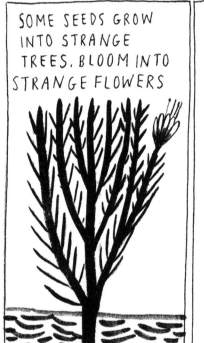

AND CREATE MORE STRANGE SEEDS THAT DISPERSE TO OTHER FARAWAY PLACES

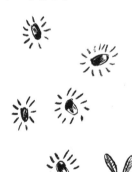

AND SOME STRANGE SEEDS BEAR STRANGE FRUIT THAT NOURISHES LIVING THINGS FOR MANY GENERATIONS.

AND SOME SEEDS ARE SO STRANGE AND WONDERFUL THEY LAY DORMANT IN THE EARTH FOR WEEKS, MONTHS, YEARS, DECADES

AND JUST WHEN YOU LEAST EXPECT IT...

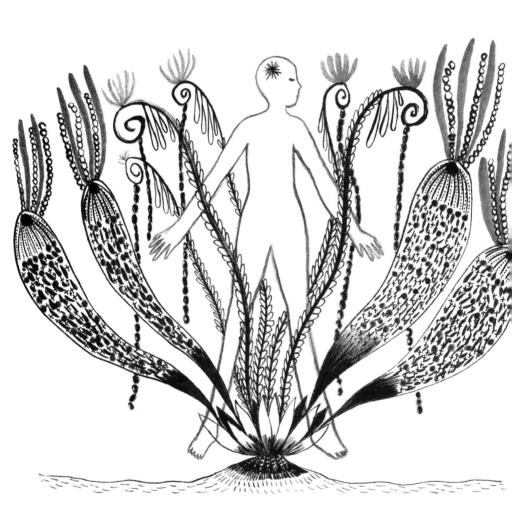

YOUR ASSIGNMENT FROM THE UNIVERSE

LESSON 5

EXPLORE YOUR INNER COSMOS

JUST AS WE ARE A PART OF
THE UNIVERSE

A UNIVERSE EXISTS WITHIN
ALL OF US

TIME TO CREATE A PORTAL TO ENTER YOUR INNER UNIVERSE...

STEP ①

LIE DOWN IN A QUIET PLACE AND CLOSE YOUR EYES

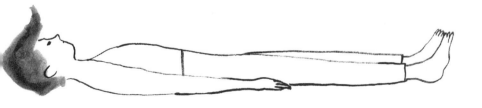

ONCE YOU HAVE FULLY
ENTERED THROUGH THE
PORTAL, BEGIN
EXPLORING

CLIMB MOUNTAIN TOPS

WALK THROUGH THE
FORESTS

SWIM THROUGH
UNDERWATER
CAVES

FEEL THE HEAT OF
NEW STARS BEING BORN

MAKE FREQUENT VISITS TO EXPLORE MORE UNCHARTED TERRITORY

IN YOUR INNER COSMOS

AS YOU RETURN FROM YOUR INNER JOURNEY YOU WILL FIND THAT THESE CLUES WILL HELP GUIDE YOU THE NEXT TIME YOU FEEL DIRECTIONLESS OR LOST

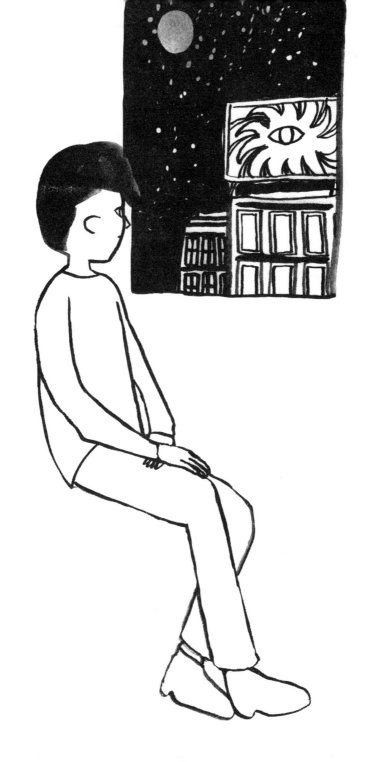

CREATE A CONSTELLATION MAP OF THE STARS YOU SEE IN YOUR INNER COSMOS

WALK ALONG A SHORELINE IN YOUR INNER COSMOS AND WRITE DOWN YOUR SECRET WISHES IN THE SAND AND WATCH THE OCEAN WAVES WASH THEM AWAY

ASK THE LIVING BEINGS OF YOUR INNER COSMOS FOR THEIR WISDOM.

WHAT IS THE ONE QUESTION YOU WISH TO ASK RIGHT THIS MOMENT?

LESSON ✳ 6

HAVE CAKE AND TEA WITH
YOUR DEMONS

THE UNIVERSE IS ONENESS

THE UNIVERSE JUST IS

SO IT IS NO WONDER THAT MANY OF US FEEL DISCONNECTED FROM THE UNIVERSE. WHEN WE SHUN OUR OWN DARKNESS (OUR WEAKNESSES, OUR ANGER, OUR SADNESS, OUR SHAME, OUR PAIN), WE ARE DISCONNECTING OURSELVES FROM THE FULL SPECTRUM OF ELEMENTS THAT EXISTS WITHIN OURSELVES AND

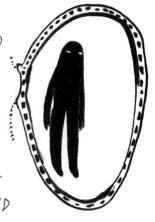

THE REST OF

THE UNIVERSE

SO LET US GET TO KNOW OUR DARKNESS, OUR DEMONS THAT EXIST IN THE DARK SHADOWS OF OUR MINDS, THE ASPECTS OF OURSELVES WE FEEL MOST ASHAMED OF

INVITE YOUR DEMON FOR A SLICE OF CAKE AND A CUP OF TEA

IT MIGHT FEEL AWKWARD AND UNCOMFORTABLE AT FIRST.

ALLOW THE DEMON TO SAY WHAT I FEELS LIKE SAYING, FEEL WHAT IT FEELS LIKE FEELING, THINK WHA IT FEELS LIKE THINKING.

SIMPLY OBSERVE AND LISTEN WITH A GENTLE INTENTION TO UNDERSTAND WHERE YOUR DEMON IS COMING FROM.

LET THE DEMON SAY WHAT IT WANTS TO SAY... AND THEN ASK YOUR DEMON TO COME BACK ANOTHER TIME FOR MORE CAKE AND TEA.

SCHEDULE REGULAR
TEA AND CAKE DATES
WITH YOUR DEMONS

SOMETIMES YOUR DEMON WILL GIVE YOU SOMETHING
IN RETURN FOR YOUR UNDERSTANDING AND KINDNESS, SOMETHING
YOU CAN ONLY RECEIVE FOR HAVING THE COURAGE TO FACE YOUR
DARKNESS. A JEWEL, A BEAUTIFUL IDEA, A KEY TO A SECRET PLACE...

AND AFTER A WHILE
YOU MAY REALIZE THAT
FOR THIS WHOLE TIME YOUR
DEMON WAS AFRAID OF YOU
AND WAS WAITING FOR
YOU THIS ENTIRE TIME

FOR YOUR LOVE,
COMPASSION, AND TIME.

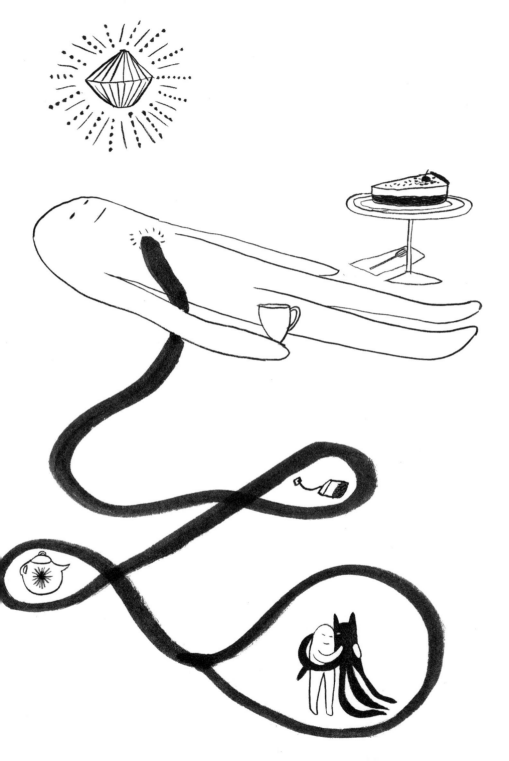

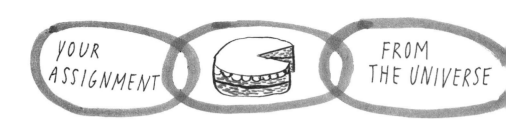

YOUR ASSIGNMENT — FROM THE UNIVERSE

✳ PREPARE DIFFERENT CAKE AND TEA COMBINATIONS FOR YOUR DIFFERENT DEMONS

for your sad demons

for your unforgiving demons

for your jealous demons

for your angry demons

✳ ONCE YOU HAVE GOTTEN TO KNOW A GOOD MAJORITY OF YOUR DEMONS, ORGANIZE A DANCE PARTY.

LESSON 7

SET YOURSELF

ON FIRE

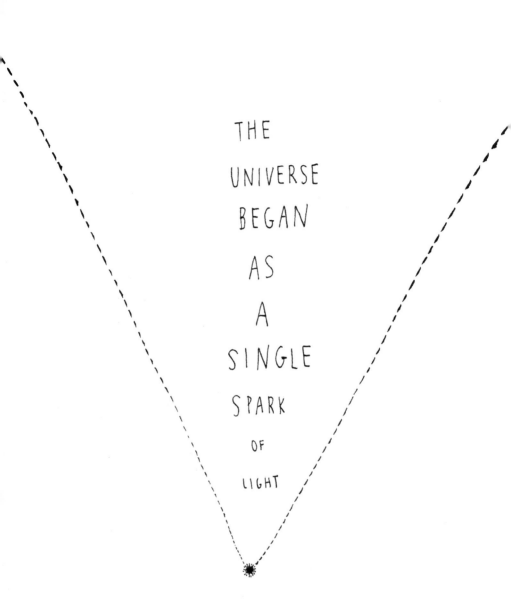

THE
UNIVERSE
BEGAN
AS
A
SINGLE
SPARK
OF
LIGHT

T THE CORE OF OUR EXISTENCE
WE ARE MADE
OF FIRE AND
LIGHT

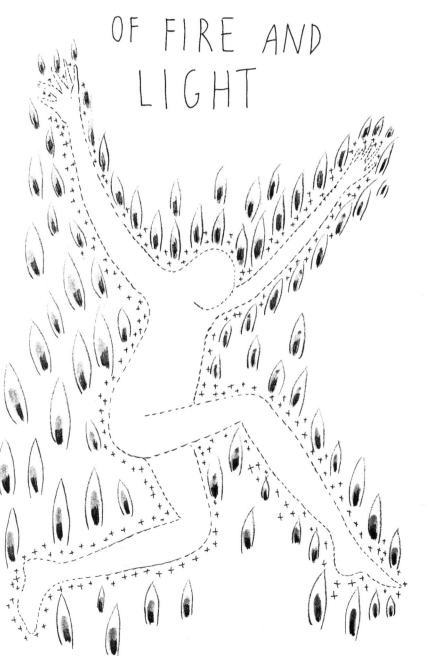

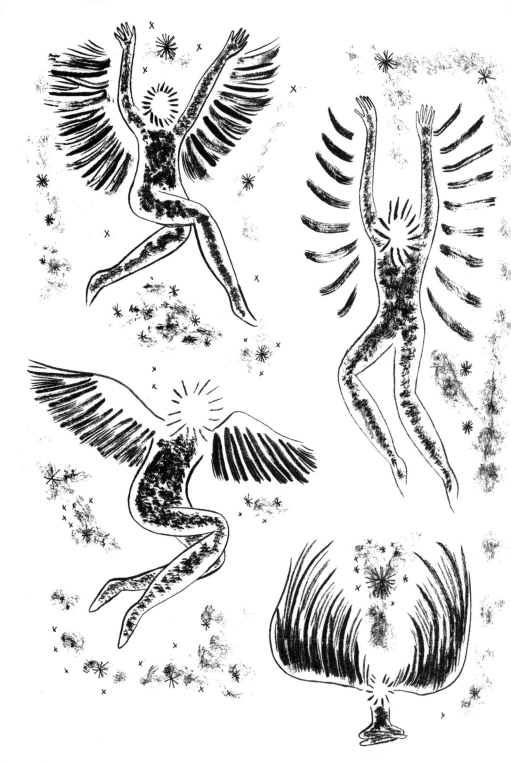

BUT OVER THE COURSE OF
OUR LIFETIME WE ACCUMULATE
JUNK AND WE BECOME IMPRISONED
BY IT

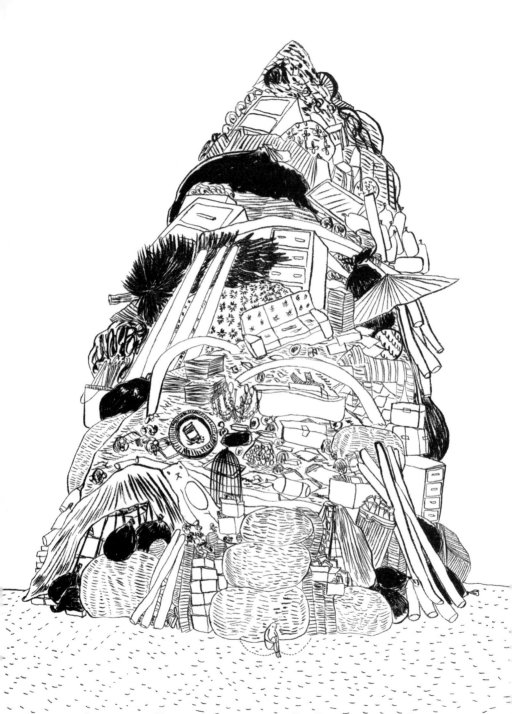

RIGHT
THIS
MOMENT

SET ON FIRE THE THINGS
YOU NO LONGER NEED

START WITH THE SMALL THINGS

YOUR ANNOYANCES

YOUR PETTY GRUDGES

YOUR DAILY STRESS

YOUR PET PEEVES

WATCH THEM LIGHT ON FIRE AND BECOME BRIGHT

AND BEAUTIFUL THINGS

THEN SLOWLY MOVE ON TO THE BIGGER THINGS LIKE YOUR PAINFUL MEMORIES YOUR CHILDHOOD ANGST YOUR UNBEARABLE GRIEF YOUR HEARTBREAK YOUR SELF-HATRED AND ANGER AT THE WORLD

SOMETIMES YOUR BURDENS ARE GODS IN
DISGUISE WAITING TO BE SET FREE
SO THEY CAN DANCE

ALLOW THE ASHES OF YOUR FORMER SELF TO SCATTER IN ALL FOUR DIRECTIONS OF THE WIND

ALL

THAT

REMAINS

IS

ALL

THAT

YOU

NEED

LESSON 8

WE ARE ALL ONE
INTERCONNECTED WEB

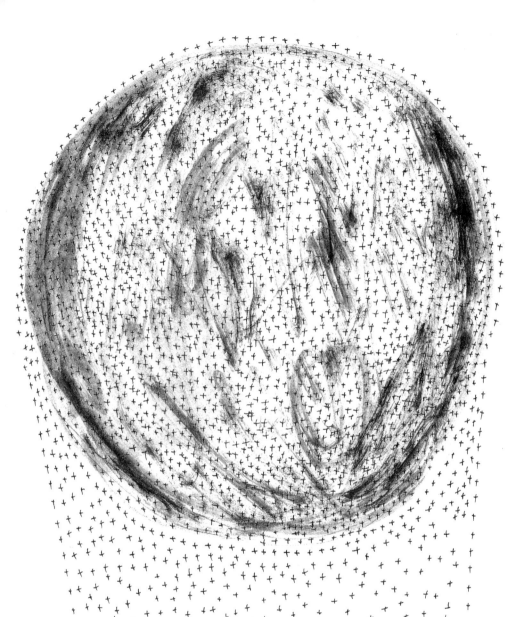

ARE YOU STILL CLINGING ONTO
YOUR EXCUSES FOR SHUTTING
YOURSELF OUT FROM THE CONNECTIONS
THAT BIND YOU TO THE REST OF THE
UNIVERSE?

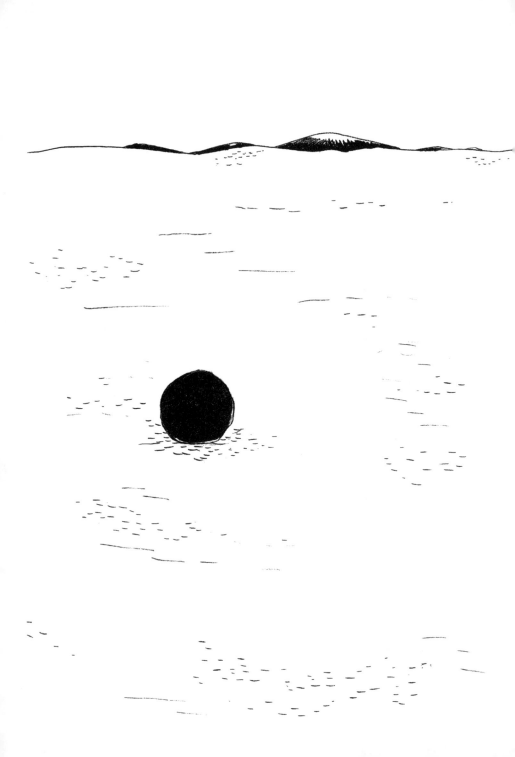

RIGHT THIS

MOMENT

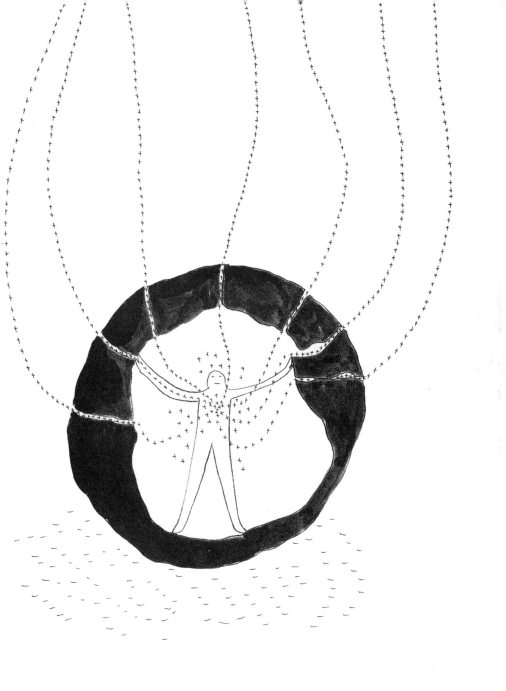

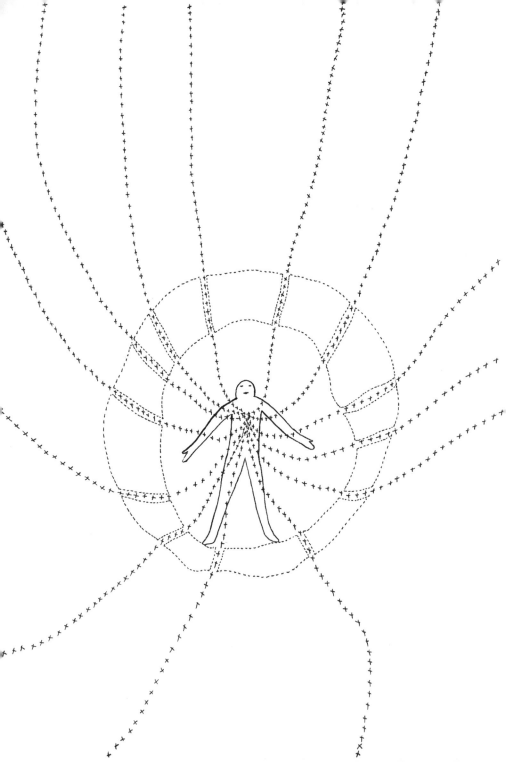

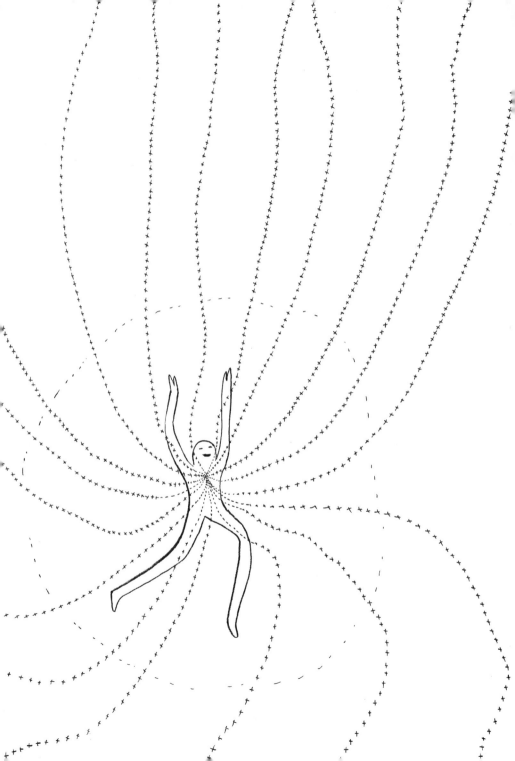

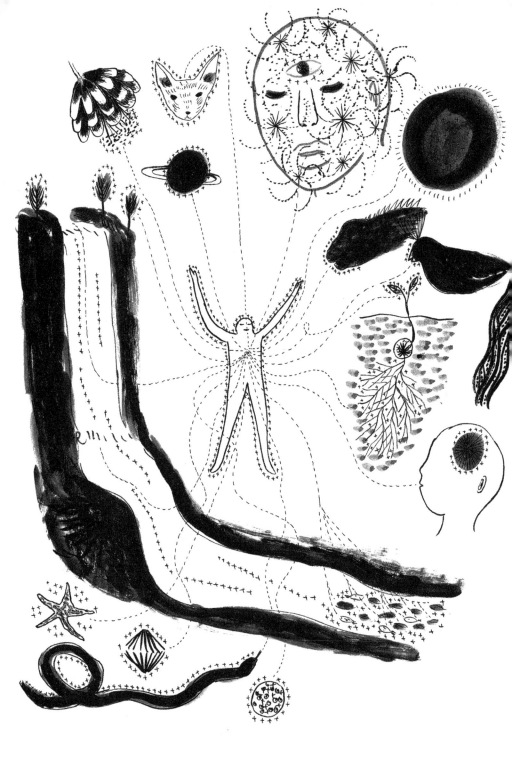

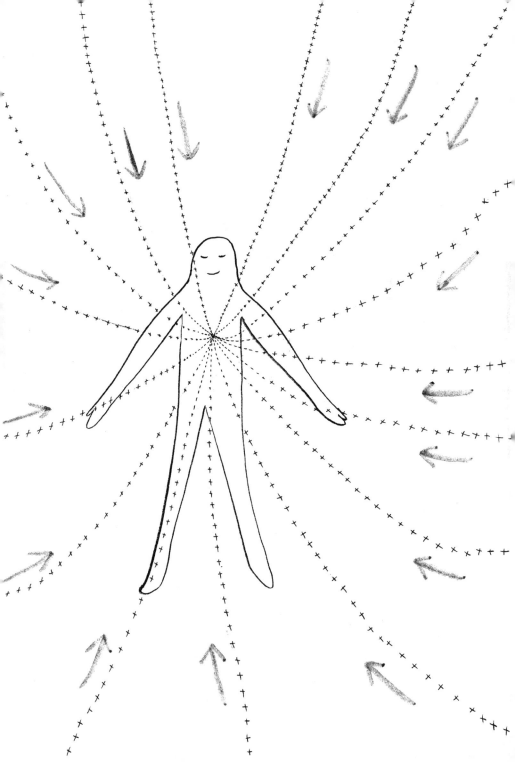

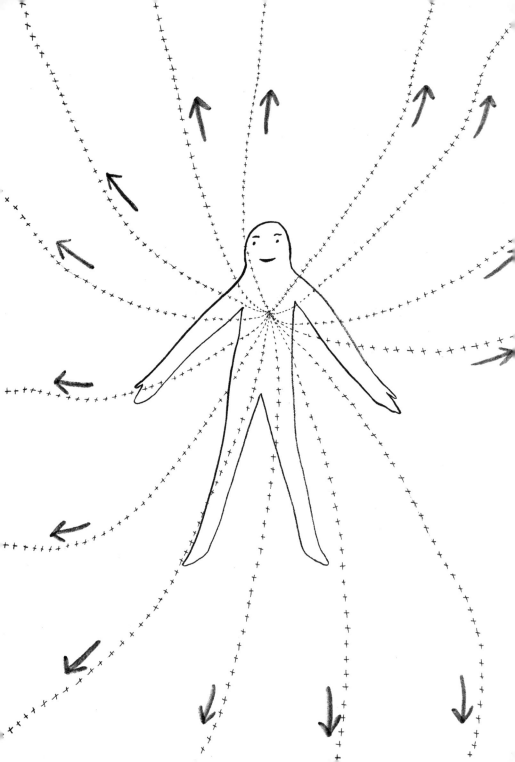

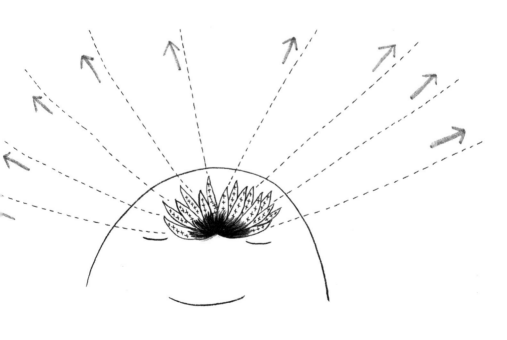

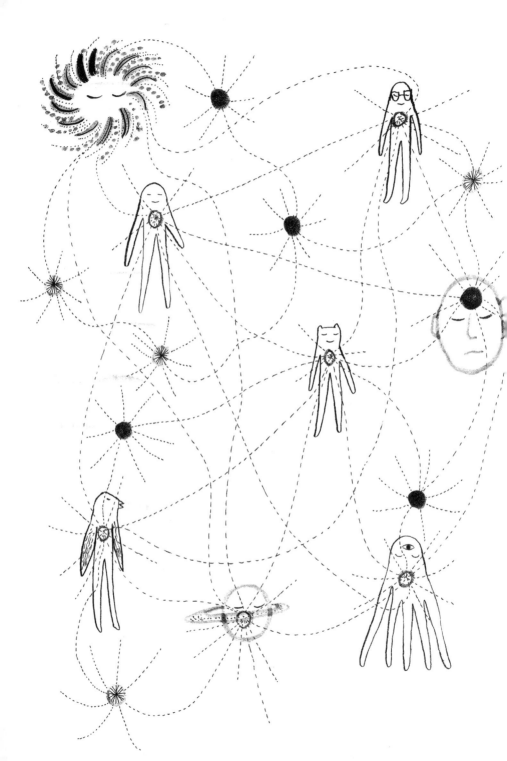

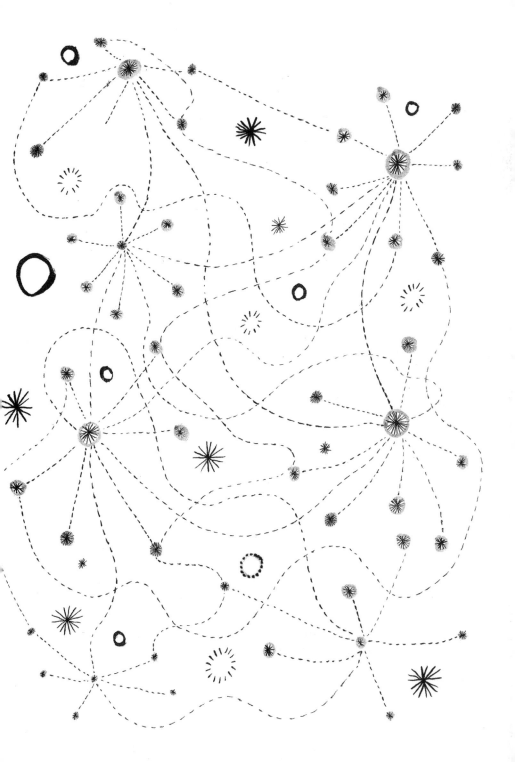

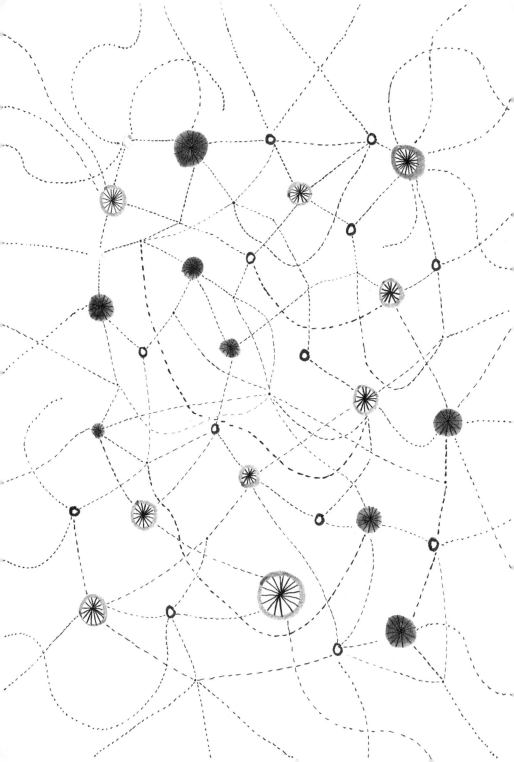

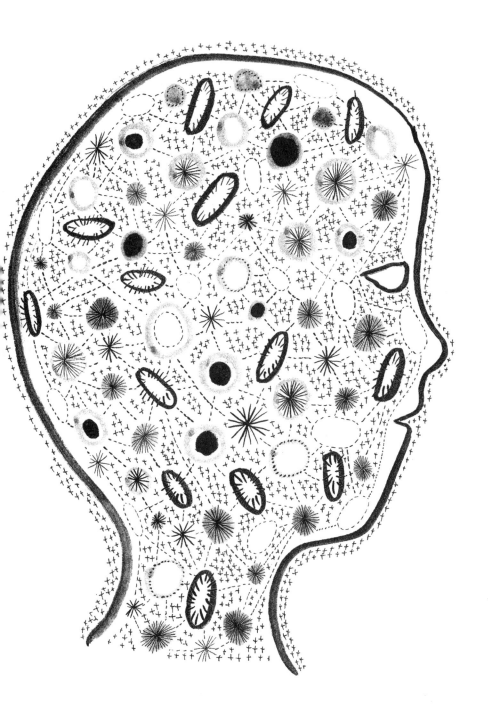

YOUR ASSIGNMENT FROM THE UNIVERSE

SIT QUIETLY FOR A MOMENT TO FEEL ALL THE *INVISIBLE THREADS* THAT CONNECT YOU TO EVERYONE IN THE UNIVERSE

SEND LOVING ENERGY
TO YOUR FAMILY, LOVED
ONES, AND FRIENDS...

... TO YOUR PERCEIVED
ENEMIES...

...TO ALL THE PEOPLE
IN THE WORLD IN PAIN...

...TO ALL THE PLANTS
AND ANIMALS ON
THIS PLANET...

TO EVERYONE ON EARTH

... AND BEYOND THE
GALAXY WE LIVE IN...

LESSON 9
ONENESS

(YOU ARE THE UNIVERSE)

AT THE ATOMIC LEVEL WE ARE MOSTLY EMPTINESS AND SPACE AND SPARKS OF ENERGY

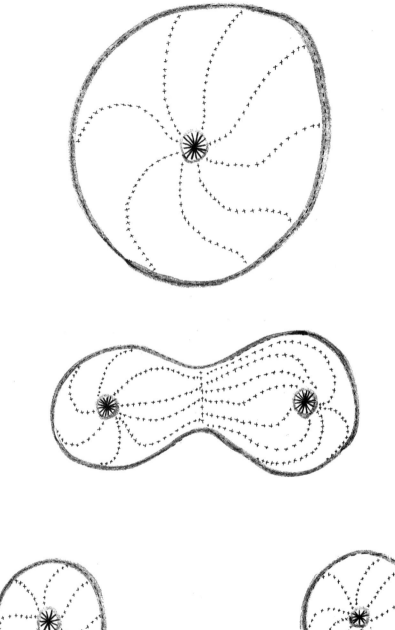
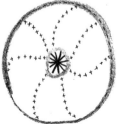
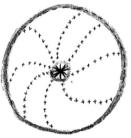

WE
EXIST
BECAUSE OF
ALL THE OTHER
LIVING CREATURES
THAT CAME BEFORE US

THERE

ARE   NO

SEPARATE

WAVES   IN   THIS

OCEAN   OF

ENERGY

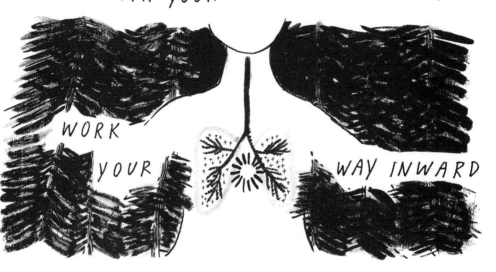

START WITH YOUR TOES AND FINGERS

WORK YOUR WAY INWARD

UNTIL THERE ARE NO BOUNDARIES BETWEEN YOU AND EVERYTHING ELSE

FEEL YOURSELF BECOME ONE WITH THE GRASS AND THE BIRDS AND THE ROCKS AND THE AIR AND THE PEOPLE AROUND YOU

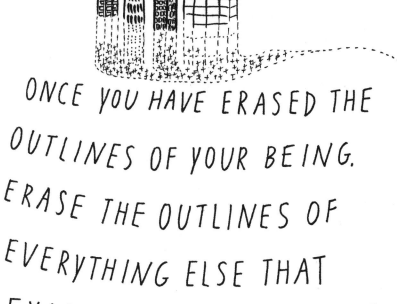

ONCE YOU HAVE ERASED THE OUTLINES OF YOUR BEING. ERASE THE OUTLINES OF EVERYTHING ELSE THAT EXISTS IN THE UNIVERSE

TO SEE
THE
UNDERLYING
ENERGY
THAT
UNITES
ALL
OF
US

YOUR ASSIGNMENT
FROM THE UNIVERSE

CREATE A NEW SPACE-TIME

CONTINUUM
OF
TRANSCENDENCE

THAT
WILL
BRING
PEACE

AND
JOY
TO
ALL
SENTIENT
BEINGS

IN THE UNIVERSE

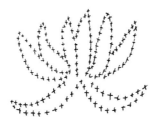

ACKNOWLEDGMENTS

I would like to express my gratitude to the following people who made this book possible.

To Stephanie Knox Cubbon for bringing so much goodness to the world and for lending me her copy of *A New Earth* by Eckhart Tolle during a particularly challenging period of my life. This book and our friendship opened my eyes for the first time to mindfulness, meditation, and separating myself from the ego.

To Mallika Chopra, founder of Intent.com, for inspiring me to manifest my intentions and for giving me the online platform to express my intentions through my art.

To my first therapist in college who reminded me again and again to be kinder to myself.

To my agent Laurie Abkemeier for her endless source of guidance and support.

To my editor Brendan O'Neill for understanding my wavelength and my language.

To all the wonderful creative individuals, communities, and independent businesses in Los Angeles and beyond who supported my self-published meditation zines and my own journey as an artist from the very beginning. Too many to name here, but I will mention: Alex and Ann Chiu of Eyeball Burp, traci kato-kiriyama and Tuesday Night Project, Jenn Witte and the amazing staff at Skylight Books, Dylan Williams and Virginia Paine of Sparkplug Books, Eric Nakamura of Giant Robot, Todd Taylor of Razorcake, L.A. Zine Fest community, and more.

To my mother and father for everything.

To my partner David Chien for always nudging me in the right direction in the universe.

ABOUT THE AUTHOR

Yumi Sakugawa is a comic book artist and the author of *I Think I Am In Friend-Love With You*. She is a regular comic contributor to The Rumpus and WonderHowTo.com, and her short comic stories "Mundane Fortunes for the Next Ten Billion Years" and "Seed Bomb" were selected as Notable Comics of 2012 and 2013 respectively by the Best American Comics series editors (Houghton Mifflin Harcourt). Her comics have also appeared in *Bitch*, *The Best American Nonrequired Reading 2014*, *Folio*, *Fjords Review*, and other publications. A graduate of the fine art program of the University of California, Los Angeles, she lives in Southern California. Visit her on the web at *www.yumisakugawa.com*.